Cute Pups
Canine Friends and Accessories

By Chie Hayano

✂ Cute Pups ☺ Contents ✂ ☺

•• ✂ Cute Pups ✂ •• Contents ••

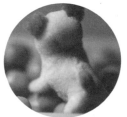

My name is
Milk

✂ Instructions ✂ ☺ **P64**

4

Milk
from Mexico

Long Coat Chihuahua: Milk

I'm finicky.
I don't like to get my
feet wet, even a little.
I mean, I'm particular
about being clean.

Shiba Inu
Hayato & Yamato
from Japan

Shiba Inu: Hayato & Yamato

We are reliable and patient. We're Japanese boys.
We learn right away how to sit and to give our paws.
Yup, that's right.

Our names are

Hayato & Yamato

✂ Instructions ✂ ☺ **P68**

DRAWING BOOK
multi-media

✂ Instructions ✂ ⊙ **P69**

My name is
John

8

Siberian Husky: John

I'm mellow.
I look mean, but I'm really sweet.
Please, don't be scared.

John
from Russia

Our names are
Moco
Neige

✂ Instructions ✂ ⊙ **P70**

Toy Poodles:
Moco & Neige

We're popular.
Aren't we fluffy?
Are our heads too big?
Do we look funny?

Moco & Neige
from France

My name is
Elf

✂ Instructions ✂ ⊙ **P71**

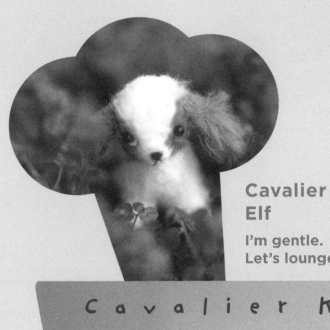

Cavalier King Charles Spaniel:
Elf

I'm gentle.
Let's lounge around and sunbathe.

Cavalier King
Charles Spaniel

Elf
from England

My name is
Friday

✂ Instructions ✂ ⊙ **P72**

Border Collie: Friday

I'm smart.
   Throw me a frisbee.
      Throw me a frisbee!
         Throw me a frisbee!!

Border Collie

Friday
from Scotland

CutePups
Playing Hardball

Dog×Dog

Hardball Staring at it, holding their ground, approaching it gingerly, grinning and thinking of doing something bad, baring their teeth and casting a fierce glance… They're pups playing hardball with many things in various situations. It's a scene you'd find anywhere with dogs.

How do they react to something that they see for the first time, or something they're used to? What do they do in that first instant when they encounter it? I can't help but think such things while observing them curiously. When I'm absent-mindedly gazing at them in a park, fascinating dramas unfold—and they can be more interesting than some of the stuff on TV.

Once, I saw a puppy chase after a stick thrown by his owner. But a crow grabbed it right from under his nose. I waited to see what would happen.

Dog×Goods

The puppy stopped dead in his tracks and faced the crow, which was way bigger than he was. In its beak was the stick that he'd been chasing up 'til then. Determined to rise to the occasion, the small puppy faced the crow and yelped bravely almost to the point of shrieking, then pounced.

But the crow escaped in a flash and nonchalantly flew off to a branch that the puppy wouldn't be able to reach. Then it moved back and forth along the branch, coming closer and almost reaching the puppy, then moving away. It was flat-out teasing the poor pup! The crow, impressed by his own cleverness, let out a gloating "Caw!" At that moment, the stick dropped down to where the puppy was crazily yelping. The puppy gleefully grabbed the stick and whizzed away. The crow seemed to droop its shoulders and glare at the puppy.

I smiled to myself. The hardball-playing puppy won!

My name is

Fango

✄ Instructions ✄ ☺ **P73**

Dalmatian: Fango

I'm so full of energy.
I can't keep my tongue from sticking out.
I'm bright-eyed and bushy-tailed.
And thirsty.

D a l m a t i a n

Fango
from Croatia

✄ Instructions ✄< ☺ **P74**

My name is
Alex

Airedale Terrier

Airedale Terrier: Alex

I'm moody.
I feel like going somewhere.
Where? Uh, out. Gotta go.

Alex
from England

21

My name is
Pocky

✂ Instructions ✂ ⊙ **P75**

Yorkshire Terrier

Yorkshire Terrier: Pocky

I'm demanding.
If you don't pay attention to me,
I'm going to chew on
your slippers.

Pocky
from England

✂ Instructions ✂ ☺ **P76**

My name is

Chappy

Maltese: Chappy

**I'm spoiled.
You know, like, uhm... What?**

M a l t e s e

Chappy
from Malta

✂ Instructions ✂ ⊙ **P77**

My name is
Kichijirou

Bulldog: Kichijirou

I'm stubborn.
What did you say?
No, I'm not going to the vet.
When I say "No," I mean it.

Bulldog

Kichijirou
from England

! A 3

≻ Instructions ≻ ⊙ **P78**

My name is
Noel

h Q ?

G

Japanese Spitz: Noel

I'm naïve.
I yelp a little if I'm surprised,
but don't get mad at me, OK?

Noel
from Japan

Japanese Spitz

1

29

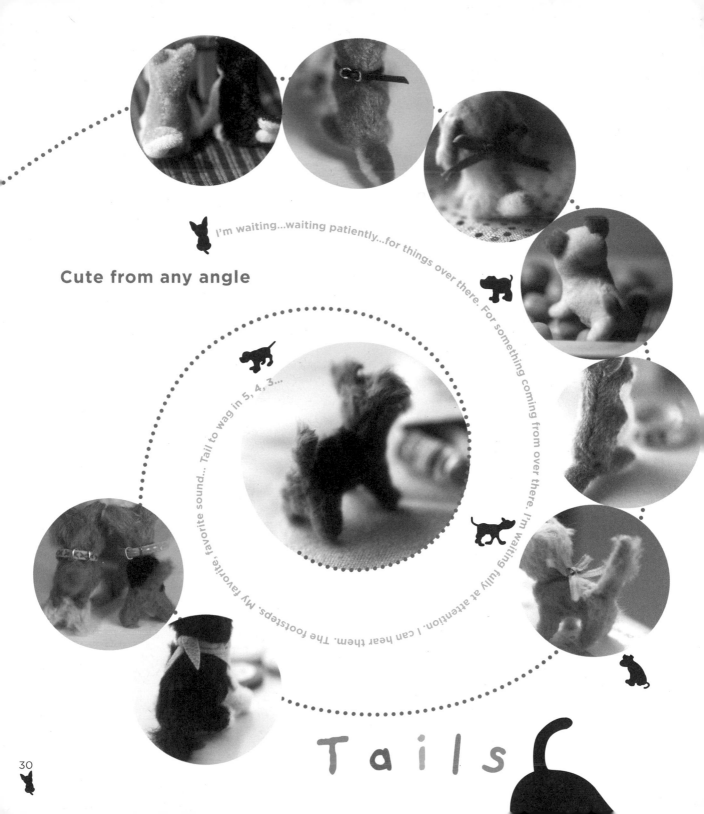

Cute from any angle

I'm waiting...waiting patiently...for things over there. For something coming from over there. I'm waiting fully at attention. I can hear them. The footsteps. My favorite. favorite, favorite sound... Tail to wag in 5, 4, 3...

Tails

30

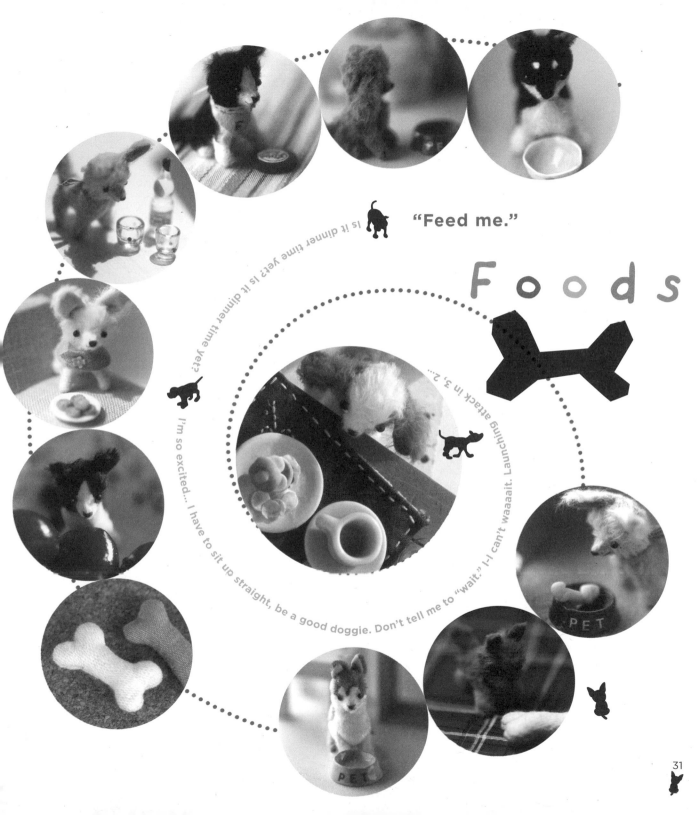

"Feed me."

Is it dinner time yet? Is it dinner time yet?

Foods

I'm so excited... I have to sit up straight, be a good doggie. Don't tell me to "wait." I-I can't waaaait. Launching attack in 3, 2...

31

Leashes

Carrier

Collars

Let's go to
the Pup Shop

Bowls

Bones

Toys

Pup Shop

Clothes

Cafe

Cushion

Carrier

Dog Bed

Opening soon!!

Sometimes it seems like these cute pups' eyes say,
"Can I have a bone?"
It's even more fun with little treats and accessories!
We opened a Cute Pup Stuff Store that specializes in
miniature-sized goods for the miniature stuffed pups.
It's OK to try things on and take pictures, but not OK to be careless
with the merchandise. Because we want to see your pup's happy face
(the happy faces of the owners, too!) do try out different items.

Cute pups that you made yourself are dear to you no matter how clumsy they may seem. Oh, I know! Let's make accessories for them!

Instructions for Accessories **Stuff for Cute Pups**

Units in the illustrations are in centimeters. (1 cm = 2/5")
Please use them as a guide but fit everything to your handmade cute pups.

First, let's make this

Collar

Materials
Appx. 6 cm of either leather or suede ribbon 2 to 3 mm wide,
2 oval jump rings (parts for jewelry)

Instructions
1. Wrap the ribbon around the dog's neck to measure, then cut ribbon to the circumference of the neck + 2 cm. Since it will be hard to wrap around the neck if it's too short, it's best to leave it long and adjust later.
2. Cut the end of the ribbon on the bias to make it easier to pull it through the jump rings. Thread the ribbon through 2 oval jump rings, and fold over approximately 8 mm. Leave one of the oval jump rings in the middle of the loop, then sew the other ring into the ribbon towards the end.

Leather or suede ribbon

Pup's neck circumference + 2 (appx. 6 total)

Cut end on the bias to make it easier to pull through

Fold over appx. 0.8

Oval jump rings

Sew to ribbon so it won't move

Put it on the pup and cut to adjust length

One More Idea!

Cut out an oval piece from a piece of aluminum, and puncture tiny holes with an awl. Inscribe the pup's name with the awl to make a name tag. Pass a jump ring through the hole, add the ring to the ribbon, and you have an original name tag.

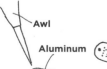

Awl

Awl

Aluminum

Pointer!

If you use suede ribbons, it'll look cute if you sew patterns with embroidery thread.

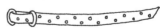

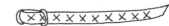

If you gave them a bone they'd be thrilled!

Bone

Materials
Polymer clay, Acrylic paint (yellow)

Instructions
1. Knead appx. 1 square cm of polymer clay, and roll it into a ball. Mix in a very small amount of acrylic paint. Continue to knead until it turns a pale yellow color.
2. Place the ball of resin clay on a flat surface and roll it into a thin log.
3. Cut log into 3 pieces, twist the edges around in a shape like the letter "e" and arrange into a bone shape, then dry or bake according to clay directions.
4. After curing, you can make the bones sturdier by coating them with matte varnish.

Knead

Roll

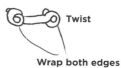
Twist
Wrap both edges

 One More Idea!

It would be fun to make them look like a real product by putting the bones in a little bag.

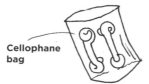
Cellophane bag

Stamp
Staple

 These items will definitely add fun to the pup's home

Cushion Bone-Shaped Cushion

Materials
Fabric of your choice, Embroidery thread, Cotton

Instructions
1. Place two pieces of fabric together reverse-side out, hold in place with marking pins, and draw the shape of a bone on one piece.
2. Sew along the line, leaving an opening to turn out.
3. Cut off the excess fabric about 2 mm from the seam, and make random incisions without cutting the seam.
4. Turn right side out through opening, stuff with cotton, and sew opening shut with ladder stitches.

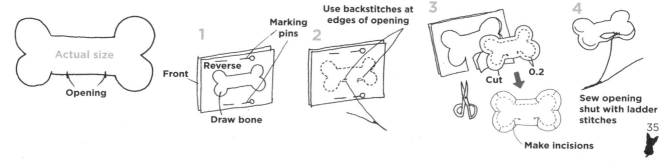

Actual size
Opening
Front
Marking pins
1 **Reverse**
Draw bone
2 Use backstitches at edges of opening
3 **Cut** 0.2
Make incisions
4 **Sew opening shut with ladder stitches**

Published by
SORAMAME

Pup Stuff Catalog

Here are various accessories and things for your cute pups.
We'll focus on various materials: paper, clay, beads, fabrics, jewelry parts, etc.
These are just a few ideas that may be nice to have for your pup.
Do you see anything you like?

Pup Stuff Catalog

The symbols in the catalog:

 Food

Clothes

 Interior Goods

 Toys

Have Fun!

Carriers

Make carriers with word-print fabric or Parisian street-map patterns. The handles are leather. The hardware makes them look so real! Add the initial of you dog's name to personalize their carrier.

Carriers

You'll get a different look with different fabrics. Here, I used polka-dot-patterned fabric for the lining to achieve a smart look. The door has a holder for a name tag. What about these for your tiny Yorkie or Maltese?

We need this! A doggie bowl.

Bowls

Materials

Stone modeling clay, Acrylic paint, Letter stencils, Varnish

Instructions

1. Take a 2 cm cube of clay (enough for 1 bowl), knead, then roll into a ball.
2. Place clay on a flat surface, and press the end of a magic marker into the middle to create an impression, then shape into a bowl. Allow to dry for one day.
3. Sandpaper the surface to smooth it into the proper shape.
4. Paint it with acrylics in any color, then allow to dry.
5. Stencil letters to spell out "DOG" or "FOOD" on the side of the bowl. Keep the overall balance in mind!
6. Add 2 coats of varnish for a glossy finish.

1 Stone modeling clay

2 Press Marker → Marker Shape & Smooth → Let it dry

3 Sand it — It's easier to sand if you use a sandpaper holder or block of wood.

4 Let's paint it red!

5 Letter stencil — Trace

6 Varnish, then let dry

Pointer!
If you want to make several bowls all the same size, I suggest using a silicone mold that can be used repeatedly.

 ## Stress buster: A toy for your pup

Toy **Frisbee**

Materials

Appx. 1.2 to 2 cm diameter button, A round, white sticker

Instructions

1. Draw a frisbee design on the sticker.
2. Place sticker so that it hides the button holes. Very simple.
   If you don't like drawing by hand, try making a design on your computer, then printing it onto a sticker or label.

 Labels

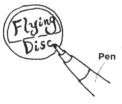 Pen — Flying Disc

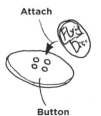 Attach — Button

 N-No way! Whee

**Cute pups need to be taken out for walks.
Let's make leashes that match their collars!**

Leash

Materials
Appx. 14 cm (5 1/2") leather or suede ribbon 2 to 3 mm wide, 3 oval jump rings, 1 jewelry clasp

Instructions
1. Use a ribbon that matches the collar.
2. Make a handle by folding one end back about 2.5 cm. Secure end with an oval jump ring and tighten ring with pliers.
3. Hook clasp through a jump ring, and thread it through the opposite end of the ribbon. Fold the ribbon back appx. 8 mm to make a loop, then add a jump ring to secure. Tighten right with pliers. Add 2 coats of varnish for a glossy finish.

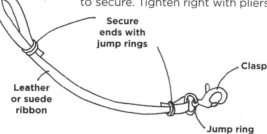

Secure ends with jump rings

Clasp

Leather or suede ribbon

Jump ring

 **There are lots of doggie clothes these days.
Your cute dogs want to be chic!**

Clothes

Materials
Micro suede, Embroidery thread, Small buttons, etc.

Instructions
Since we are using micro suede which doesn't fray, it's very simple to make these outfits. Let's make a bunch and play dress-up!

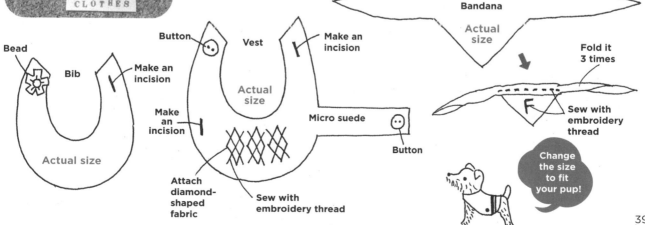

Bandana
Actual size

Fold it 3 times

Sew with embroidery thread

Button

Vest

Make an incision

Make an incision

Actual size

Micro suede

Button

Bead

Bib

Make an incision

Make an incision

Actual size

Attach diamond-shaped fabric

Sew with embroidery thread

Change the size to fit your pup!

Pup Stuff Catalog

 ### Cushion

These are adorable! Cushions shaped like bones! Once you've made these you'll want to try making all kinds of little goods for your cute pups. It's so much fun choosing which fabrics to use for all the fun little accessories.

Bones

"I want a bone! I want a bone!" Modeled after a certain cartoon character's favorite bone. If you make this for your pup he'll be totally blissed out! Curling up the ends is kinda hard, though.

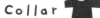

 ### Dog Bed

For cute dogs only: a dog bed. Make the section where they sit fluffy and comfortable with stuffing. The backrest is made of soft felt material. My goodness, it's so luxurious. For your information, I myself sleep on a flat, hard futon.

Collar

This is the first accessory to make for your new pup. Putting a collar on a dog is a little ritual, as if to say, "Here you go, now you belong with us." When they're this tiny, though, it's just too cute.

 Clothes

Make a vest, bib, or bandana for your dog using colorful micro suede which doesn't fray. These are so easy to make. I added accents by embroidering patterns—argyle, stripes, or initials.

Toys

This is the simplest toy: the frisbee. I made it in about 5 seconds after choosing from buttons I had lying around. Draw on a sticker, stick it to the button, and that's it! Now, would your cute pup play fetch if you threw it?

 Leashes

Pups need to be walked. Wouldn't it be nice to match it to the collar and make them into a set? Like, what color leash would you like to wear today? Oh, you don't need that many? The question is: would your cute dog go out for a walk on a leash?

Bowls

A necessity, right? I was very particular about their shape. After molding the stone clay, sand it with sandpaper. You need 3 years' practice before you can make them perfectly (kidding).

41

I'm going to make a bed for my pup,
even though I sleep on a futon.

Dog Bed (Size: length 4.5 cm x width 5.5 cm x height 2.5 cm)

Materials
Thin cardboard, Felt, Fabrics, Stuffing, Embroidery thread

Instructions
1. Cut out parts A and B from cardboard. These are the cores for the base and backrest. Make incisions on B and mark the folding line. Prepare fabric (a) for the cushion cover, felt (b) for the backrest, and felt (c) for the bottom.
2. Attach a small amount of stuffing to one side of cardboard A with glue, wrap it with fabric (a), fold over incised edges towards the back, then glue edges to secure.
3. With the reverse side out, sew sides of felt (b) making sure cardboard B can fit inside. Turn right-side out and insert cardboard B. Glue together cardboard B and felt (b) with glue.
4. With the longer edge of the backrest facing out, wrap it around the cushion from step 2, and glue together.
5. Glue felt (c) underneath to cover the base.
6. Sew the lower edges of the bottom and the outside of the backrest with embroidery thread in a similar color.

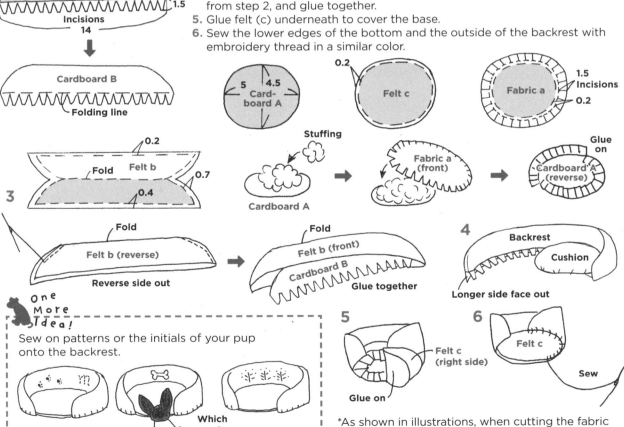

One More Idea!

Sew on patterns or the initials of your pup onto the backrest.

Which one's mine?

*As shown in illustrations, when cutting the fabric and felt, please add seam margins to the fabric and extra allowances to the size of the cardboard pieces.

I always wanted a carrier just like this one

Carrier

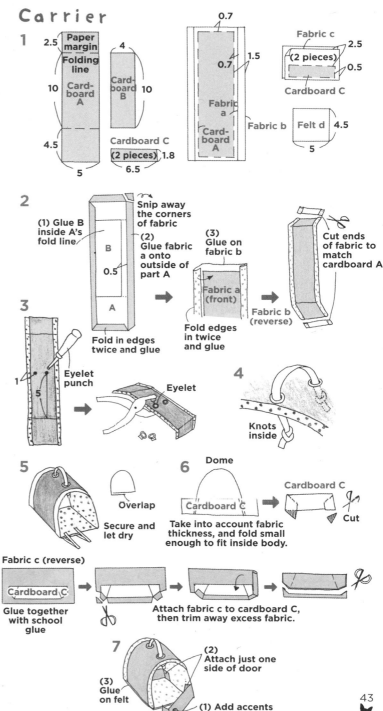

Materials

Thin cardboard, 2 types of fabrics,
2 eyelets,
Appx. 7 cm of leather ribbon 3 to 4 mm wide,
Felt, Buttons or beads for accents

Instructions

1. Cut parts A, B, and C from cardboard and mark A with 2 fold lines using the back of a knife blade. Prepare fabric (a) for the outside of the dome and fabric (b) for the inside. Fabric (c) is for the door, and felt (d) for gluing it on the bottom.

2. (1) Layer cardboard B over A, and glue together (to reinforce the dome). Part B will be the inside of the dome.
   (2) Glue fabric (a) onto outside of cardboard A.
   (3) Glue fabric b onto cardboard B. Fold edges on the long sides in twice to create a border on the front of A. Cut short ends to match cardboard A.

3. With an eyelet punch, create 2 holes on the center of the dome. These will hold the handle. If the holes are too small, widen them with an awl, then add eyelets.

4. Thread leather ribbon through the holes, and tie knots inside to secure.

5. Curve cardboard A into a dome, fold margin and bottom together to create a floor, and glue together. Secure with clothespins, etc. until completely dried.

6. Fold the edges of cardboard C so that it fits inside the dome. Trim away lower parts at ends to make folding easier. Next, glue fabric (c) onto cardboard C. Trim away extra fabric. Repeat, creating 2 doors.

7. (1) Sew on buttons, beads, etc. onto the door. It's also cute to add a name tag holder.
   (2) Glue doors to the body.
   (3) Glue felt (d) to the base.

43

Shall we take a little break?

A bright red, spiffy toy for spirited Fango, and a cute one with polka dots for aggressive Kichijirou. They seem to like their new toys. Their tongues lolling out are too adorable!

Are we cool or what?

How do we look?

Dude, I look great.

Do you like our new collars?

Collection

Quickly!

Collect them all!

I like to hide under them.

Fango turns everything into a toy.
Today's game is "Digging for Treasure."
Now, what is Kichijirou doing?
Playing "Hide and Seek?" I can seeeeee you!

Peek-a-boo?

Can you guess who?

Peek-a-boo!

I'm Kichijirou!

Soramame's Diary

Part
One

No.001

46

No. 001

The eyes stick out oddly, the ears have gaping holes, and there is a piece of felt in bright red...is it a nose or a mouth? The tail is almost falling off, hanging by a thread to the body. This scary object is, in fact, the memorable No. 001, the very first stuffed animal that I made.

I think it was when I was a first-grader. Back then, glove puppets made from cotton work gloves were all the rage. I loved the 5-finger pig puppets that my mom used to make for me. "I want to make one!" I insisted, and chose to make a mouse, since it appeared to be the simplest. I cut the finger off a glove and stuffed it. What finally materialized—after poking myself with a needle countless times—was a patchy, Frankenstein-like thing. Precocious child that I was, convinced that I had deft fingers and that I should be able to make anything skillfully, I was shocked by the sore sight of the outcome. This was followed by a temper tantrum: I shrieked and tossed it into the trash can. Even when my mom said, "After all the effort that you put into making it! I think it's charming." But I didn't look at it again. I said I didn't like it and that it wasn't cute at all, and was mad at myself for not being able to do it well.

That mouse, which would have become garbage, is sitting here now. The mouse, which was secretly rescued from the trash by my mom, caught my eye later on when I was calmer. Somehow I began to feel really bad for it and changed my mind, thinking, "In its own way, it's kinda cute."

As time passed, I would occasionally think, "Okay, maybe it's time to toss it out," but every time the mouse looked at me with its sad, wonky eyes, stopping me from throwing it away.

I can't let it go now. I'll gently put it back in its box. There's some sort of special feeling that stays with the very first thing you've ever made.

The top three things on Pocky's list,
"Things that have been on my mind recently."
(1) Milk, who is rumored to be better-looking than me
(2) Foods that my owner likes
(3) Where I hid that bone
Right now, I'm thinking about (2).

Prodding

!   Here we go!   Pull!

I'm spoiled

Take me out for a walk!   Take me out, now!

I'm greedy

!

I'm bored with the same food everyday
(but I still eat it).

These look yummy!

'm gonna take this so we can go for a walk.

Eh? Why's it so heavy?

Oh, you were stepping on it! Hee hee.

A Tiny, Tiny Story

Warm, fluffy and happy

Alex knows that if he takes that leash, the front door will open and he can go outside. Alex knows if he takes this without permission, even though his owner gets mad, she'll secretly be pleased.

Soramame's Diary

Dear Chiro

About Chiro

I've never owned a real dog. Although I used to dream about becoming a vet or working at a zoo, before I knew it I'd become a salaried office worker. I haven't fulfilled my dream of owning a dog yet, because I live in a small apartment. Since I'm envious of people who own dogs, I always try to get close and pet any dog I see. Of all such dogs, Chiro was a very special pup to me. She was a Pomeranian that lived with my grandparents that was at least twice as big as a regular-sized Pomeranian. Although I was only able to see her once or twice a year, she always gave me a big, enthusiastic welcome whenever I went over. I even got to take her for walks. In the morning, I awoke to the sound of Chiro's light, clicky footsteps along the corridor. Behind the door, Chiro seemed to have sensed that I was awake. Her footsteps would grow more and more animated, as if she was doing a tap dance. When I finally opened the door, there stood the grinning Chiro, who jumped and bounced, and said "Good morning!" by brushing up against my feet. Every day started like that, and I spent most of the time at my grandparents' house hanging out with Chiro. Her round forehead, doe eyes, and tongue with a slightly rough surface, hind legs stretched out as she lay flat on her stomach, little ears that reacted to the voice of my grandfather, and somewhat unruly, tangled fur. The hiding place for snacks, midday sirens that Chiro hated, and favorite stops along the walking route. Everything delighted me, and I followed Chiro around, almost to the point of annoying her. The first little pooch that I made with mohair fabric was modeled after Chiro. I diligently sewed, thinking as I worked Chiro's quirks. If Chiro never existed, I probably would never have thought, "I want to make mini stuffed animals!" and I never could have done it, either.

Now Chiro rests in a grave alongside my grandparents and our ancestors. All my relatives invariably offer incense sticks to Chiro as well, reminding me that each one of them has memories of Chiro. It's been more than 10 years since she passed away, but Chiro is still the special pup that I really cared about for the first time, and she became the inspiration for my mini cute pups!

Snacking Buddies

A Tiny, Tiny Story

Pocky is the type that likes to keep snacks all to himself.
While he's standing his ground with Alex,
Kichijirou nabs a snack of his own.

Mine!

No, these are mine!!

What about this?
--That's mine, too!!

I'm taking these...

He's staring at me. He's really staring at me.
What's behind his gaze?
What kind of stories are going to unfold in the days to come?
Now, why don't you come up with your own stories for
your cute dogs?

In Love

I-It's Friday from next door.

Staring...

Oh no! He saw me!

A baby chick?

?

Did it hatch yet?

Hurry, let me out of here!

Soramame's Diary

Photo
Shoots

54

About the Photo Shoots

If I were asked what the most fun part of making cute pups is, all in all, I'd have to say, "taking pictures." It's really fun when I'm brushing the finished dogs and paying attention to the details and the set. I move the little props around, or change the angles of the pups. It's like playing house, really.

Each time I look through the viewfinder, I smile to myself.

I usually shoot them out on the veranda before noon when I have a day off. But since I need to set the cute pups on a platform, I usually use the tops of my 3 parrots' cages. The cages are all slightly different, so when I want a varied setting, they're perfect. So we all head out to the veranda, no matter if it's hot or cold outside.

When I place a platform over the cages, the parrots cock their heads and seem to say irritably, "What? What's this? What are these things above our cages?!" As I get in the zone while shooting, sometimes the most aggressive of my parrots, Mr. Blue, will suddenly peck at my legs. Oh, boy, that was close. Gotta watch out!

Welcome to
Soramame Studio

Soramame Studio

When I first start on a project, my work place is always a mess. It's so messy with open paint tubes over there, a piece of half-cut wood over here, and the surrounding areas covered with all the little things needed for making cute pups. I pull out materials and tools from here and there, and it all becomes a giant, crazy mess. I thought it was getting out of hand, so I began a studio restructuring project. I wanted everything within easy reach so I could hunker down and work. I want to be like the old man with six arms from a famous anime, where I can swiftly grab tools and things without looking, while smoothly proceeding with my work! I painted some shelving, added work lights, and created a closet-sized studio. Here I can concentrate easily and work for long hours. But once I started working, things began to creep up on the table, under the table, around the table... Oh, to be good at organizing!

Snip, Snip, Snip

Favorite Things & Books

Favorite Photobooks

"Dog Dogs" by Elliott Erwitt portrays the humorous relationships between dogs and humans. I love it. The tongue-in-cheek viewpoint of the author and photographer makes me laugh out loud.

"A Traveler's Cat-like Sentiments" Photo album by Shuji Aizawa and Kyoko Aizawa, published by Éditions Treville,

"Cats in the Sun" Published by Éditions Treville. Although these books are by different authors, both contain numerous photos that illustrate the lives of cats. Somehow, when I gaze at them, I feel like rethinking my life. Cats are picturesque no matter how they pose.

"Today's Dogs 2" Published by Oumi Publishing. "Today's Dogs" is one of my favorite TV shows. Now that it's a book, I can look through it whenever I want. When I reread it occasionally, it goes straight to my heart and relaxes me.

"138 Dog Breeds" from Nihon Bungeisha. I just bought this book recently. It has tons of info about various dogs—some I've never heard of before. Even pups of the sam breed can look totally different!

Cute Pups

Instructions

In this book, all the patterns for cute pups are based on Milk's pattern. I will show how to create the other breeds later on. They are all hand-sewn, and the patterns are at 100%. Since the patterns include seam margins, sew 1/16" (1 to 2 mm) from the edge. Aside from the materials listed, you'll need stuffing, thread, and stainless steel balls. Please allow for extra fabric when measuring. Most of the materials for making cute pups are available from fabric shops or stores that carry materials for making teddy bears.

Basic sewing techniques

Since they're small, each pup is hand-sewn.

Half-Backstitch

Use the half-backstitch for stitching pieces of fabric together. Use 1/15" (1 to 3 mm) stitches. At the beginning and at the end of the stitches, always go back one stitch.
Make a French knot at the end, scoop up one stitch and draw the thread, hiding the knot.

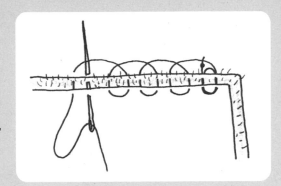

Figure-8 Knot

For stitching the tip of the snout, under the jaw, and stitching together two edges of fabric, use a figure-8 knot. This way, the pieces will stay aligned. Use smaller stitches for the snout and the legs since they tend to unravel when turning out the fabric or adding stuffing.

Ladder Stitch

When closing an opening, take the same stitch alternately through abutted fabric. While pushing in the stuffing with the needle to keep it inside, sew the fabric together so that the thread forms a reversed "C."

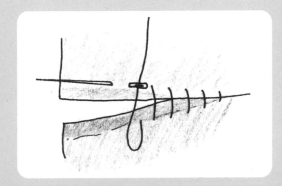

For Cute Pups

Materials and Tools

Plyester thread No. 60 (for plain seams)

Strong and flexible. Easy to use; recommended for those who have a hard time using transparent nylon thread.

Embroidery thread, machine thread No. 50 Black (for accents)

Used for noses and mouths. I use machine thread No. 50 (black) that has a slight sheen to it. Of course, embroidery thread works, too.

Transparent nylon thread (for plain seams)

Can be used with any type of fabric, and since it's transparent, it won't spoil the look. Although tricky to use at first, it's very convenient.

Faux (viscose) fur

Fabric with pile depth of appx. 1/8" (3 to 5 mm). Used when making long-haired dogs. Since faux fur frays more easily compared to fleece (especially when sewing or turning out), treating the raw edges with diluted glue will make it easier to handle.

Miniature fur

Or micro fleece. Soft fabric with pile depth of appx. 1/16" (1 to 3 mm). This fabric doesn't fray easily, and is easy to sew. It also comes in a variety of colors.

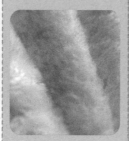

Mohair

Pile depth is appx. 1/3" (1 cm), and here, I use it for the Spitz. Select fabric that is as dense as possible.

Faux Suede

Used for the insides of ears, tongue, and clothes. Thin and easy to handle. There's no need to treat the edges. Comes in a variety of colors. There are different types such as ultra and micro suede, and I've sorted them by color.

Stainless steel balls

In order to give the dogs stability and weight, I wrap about 15 to 20 balls into the stuffing. I use small ones, appx. 3 mm in diameter.

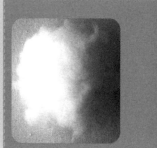

Synthetic stuffing

Pull off small clumps and squeeze into little pieces before stuffing.

Onyx beads

Round beads. Most need 2 mm beads (for the Bull Terrier, use 1.5 mm). Sizes vary by brand, so use whatever's available, and enjoy how each dog's expression is different.

Glass eyes

Use 2 mm for the Siberian Husky. Loop the wire with a pair of pliers, insert, and secure by sewing.

Wood Glue

Coat the raw edges of easily frayed fabric with diluted glue. This makes fabric easier to work with.

Needle

Thin needles. I use a fine, silk thread needle.

Pliers

Used when cutting or bending wires for glass eyes or when adding jump rings to the collar or leash.

Awl
Thin type used for crafting. Used for punching holes where eyes are to be placed, or when pulling out pile that got caught in the seams.

Forceps
Although forceps are a surgical tool, they're very convenient when turning out pieces or when stuffing the dogs. If forceps aren't available, use marking pins or a set of tweezers.

Scissors
A sharp pair with narrow blades.

Toothbrush
Used for brushing.

For
Accessories

Materials and Tools

Felt
Used in dog beds and carriers.

Ribbons (leather, suede, etc.)
1/16 to 1/8" (1.5 to 4 mm) wide. Used for making collars, leashes and handles of carriers.

Beads, Small Buttons, etc.
Add to clothes, carrier doors, toys, etc.

Fabric
Any color. Used in cushions, dog beds, etc.

Eyelets
Used to reinforce the holes' handles. Use ones that are about 1/8" (4 mm) in diameter.

Jump rings, jewelry clasps
Used in collars and leashes.

Acrylic paints
Used for painting cured clay pieces.

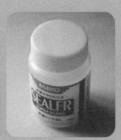

Varnish
For finishing bones and bowls.

Clay
Polymer clay is used for making bones, and stone modeling clay for bowls.

Cardboard
Used as a core for dog beds and carriers.

Ruler, X-Acto knife
Used for cutting cardboard and creating fold lines.

Instruction Pointers

① Placing the pattern and cutting the fabric

Take note of the grain (or fur) direction. There's an arrow on each pattern to indicate the grain line. Also, when there are 2 separate pieces for the torso and the ears, reverse the pattern so that the pieces are symmetrical. The patterns include seam margins. Sew appx. 1 to 2 mm from the raw edges. For the legs and tip of the snout, keep appx. 2 mm of seam margin when sewing.

② Treating the raw edges of faux fur and mohair

Since they tend to fray, keep larger seam margins (2 to 3 mm). Treating the edges of the fabric will make it easier to work with. Dilute wood glue with a small amount of water, coat the edges with a brush, and let dry.

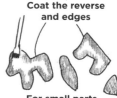

Glue

Water

Glue

Dissolve

Coat the reverse and edges

For small parts, coat everything

③ Small parts

Since the white parts for the eyes and eyebrows are very small, I cut them right before attaching so as not to lose them. Since it's difficult to cut out small parts when holding the fabric, cut out the pieces with a little extra allowance, impale it on a needle or a marking pin, then cut off the excess.

④ How to attach tongues and eyebrow dots

Tongue: Insert the needle from the back of the neck, and pull out below the nose, under the embroidered mouth. Slide tongue piece over needle to under the nose. Insert needle through tongue and pull out behind an ear. Tug thread so the center of the tongue curves in, then secure thread with a knot. Eyebrow dots: Insert the needle from the back of the head, and pull the thread out where you want the eyebrow dot. If you insert the needle back into the middle of the eyebrow dot and draw the thread towards the back of the head, the eyebrow dot will sink in and it'll look smaller.

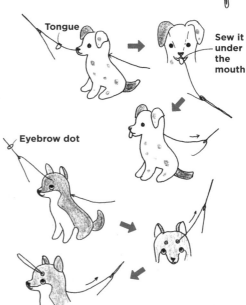

Tongue

Sew it under the mouth

Eyebrow dot

⑤ Droopy ears

After attaching ears, bend ear, then sew the tip to the head.

Sew

6 Coat patterns

The coat patterns such as patches are sewn on like appliqués. Since they are so small, it's tough to stitch together the patterns—especially curves—with the fabric inside-out. Like an appliqué, place the pattern piece over the body fabric, and use small cross-stitches to lock in the edges of the pattern piece. Now there are 2 layers of fabric which makes it hard to turn out, so cut off the section of the fabric underneath the pattern piece leaving appx. 2 mm of seam margin.
Also, when sewing together sections with patterns or patches such as the body and the head, make sure that the colors match. Reinforce abutted areas by doubling up stitches.

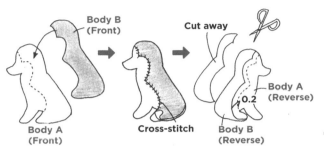

Body B (Front)
Cut away
Body A (Reverse)
Cross-stitch
Body B (Reverse)
0.2
Body A (Front)

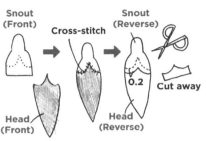

Snout (Front)
Cross-stitch
Snout (Reverse)
Head (Front)
0.2
Cut away
Head (Reverse)

For abutted fabric, match edges, and double up stitches.
Reverse

7 Curled tails

To make a curled tail, fold lightly along the placement line and sew the opening closed. Don't stuff the tail. Close the opening on the back of the body part way. Insert the tail so that the seam faces upward. Once you finish stuffing the rear, cross-stitch the tail in place. Without cutting the thread, pull out where the tail joins the back, insert the needle through the tip of the tail (point A), then insert it again where the tail joins the back, thread through the rear, and secure with a knot.

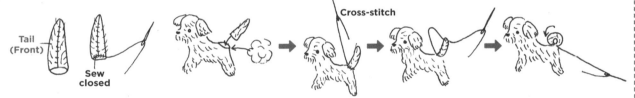

Tail (Front)
Sew closed
Cross-stitch

8 If legs are too far apart

When stuffing the legs, work gradually, starting with the tips. After sewing everything together, insert needle under a foreleg and out from under the opposite foreleg, then pass through again to the first side. Tightly pull thread, then secure with a knot.

9 Finishing

Pull out the pile from under the seams with an awl and brush the coat with a toothbrush. Careful brushing will produce a beautiful coat, and will make all the difference.

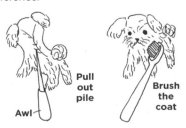

Pull out pile
Awl
Brush the coat

Milk

Milk Instructions
Long Coat Chihuahua

She's sticking her little head out of her carrier and looking around restlessly with a helpless look on her face. Isn't she adorable?

Instructions

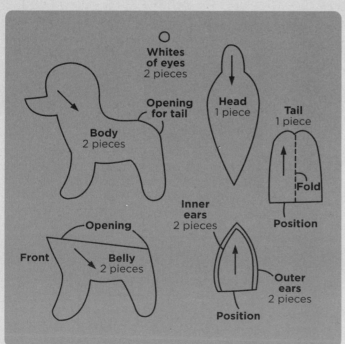

Whites of eyes
2 pieces

Opening for tail

Head
1 piece

Tail
1 piece

Body
2 pieces

Fold

Position

Opening

Inner ears
2 pieces

Front

Belly
2 pieces

Outer ears
2 pieces

Position

Materials

Body, belly, head, outer ears, tail:
faux (viscose) fur (white)
Inner ears: micro fleece (pink)
Whites of eyes: micro suede (white)
Pupils: onyx beads

Pointers!

Wide-spaced eyes, large ears

Treatment of fabric:
Refer to Instruction Pointer 2
Whites of eyes:
Refer to Instruction Pointer 3
Tail: Stuff the tail

Milk Instructions
Photo p. 4

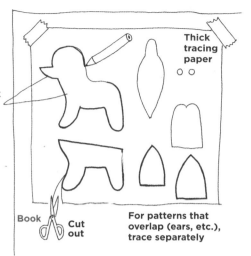

After tracing patterns, mark each piece

Thick tracing paper

Book — Cut out

For patterns that overlap (ears, etc.), trace separately

1 Make the patterns

Lay a thick piece of tracing paper on the patterns, secure it so that it won't move, then trace the patterns with a pencil. For those with overlapping patterns such as outer ears and inner ears, trace patterns separately, write down on each the grain line, opening, names of parts, and the number of pieces needed. Cut out the patterns with a pair of sharp scissors following the line.

2 Mark the fabric

Lay patterns next to each other on the reverse side of the fabric, paying attention to the grain direction. Mark the fabric with a fine ball-point pen or pencil. Don't forget to flip the pattern for symmetrical parts such as the chest, patches and ears. Also mark the fabric with notches for the openings, etc.

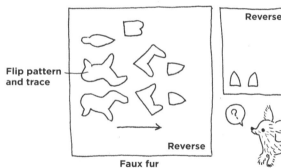

Flip pattern and trace

Reverse

Faux fur

Reverse

Micro fleece

3 Cut the fabric

With a pair of narrow, sharp scissors, cut little by little so you don't cut the pile.

4 Treating the raw edges of fabric

Coat the raw edges of the reverse side of the fabric with diluted glue and let dry. This will make it easier to handle, and makes the fabric resistant to fraying. I recommend brushing it on lightly; if it's too thick, the fabric will be too stiff, and that makes it hard to work with.

5 Sew

Sew together each piece. Use half-backstitches for sewing pieces together and ladder stitches when closing an opening.
(1) First, place the front sides of the body pieces facing each other, then sew under the jaw from point A to point B. When you reach point B, which is the tip of the snout, (2) firmly secure the head piece using a figure-8 knot.
(3) Sew to point C at the back of the head. (4) Next, sew the other side from the tip of the snout, point B, through point C, up to point D, which is the opening for inserting the tail.
Sew together the body and the belly starting from point A under the jaw. (5) Sew both the left side and the right side starting at point A and ending at point E. If any pile sticks out as you sew, push it in with the needle and continue. (6) Sew the belly pieces together just from under the jaw to the edge of the opening.

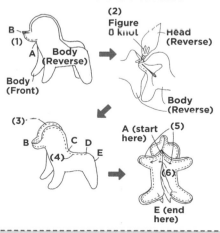

B (1)
A
Body (Front)
Body (Reverse)

(2) Figure 0 knot — Head (Reverse)
Body (Reverse)

(3)
B
C D
E
(4)

A (start here) (5)
(6)
E (end here)

Milk Instructions

6 Turn it out

If the fabric is too stiff from the glue, loosen it by kneading. Turn out little by little through the opening. Don't try to do it all at once; go slowly. Once you get it as far as possible by hand, use forceps or a pin to turn it out by pushing out the head first, then legs and the tip of the snout. Work slowly. For delicate parts, scoop the fabric with a marking pin to pull it out.

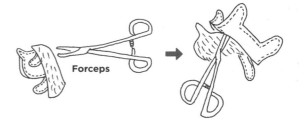

Forceps

7 Stuffing

Tear off small portions of stuffing little by little. Starting with the snout, stuff it gradually by using forceps or a set of tweezers. Unless you stuff it firmly, it'll be hard to give it an expression later on. After firmly stuffing the head, stuff the feet. After stuffing the feet, insert 2 marking pins through the base of the legs. Arrange the legs and body into the shape it should be once it's finished, then stuff. Sew the opening halfway closed with ladder stitches. For the final part, wrap appx. 10 to 15 stainless steel balls into stuffing to give the body some weight. This way, it's stable and has presence. Sew closed opening (to point E).

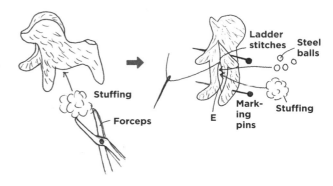

Stuffing

Forceps

Ladder stitches

Steel balls

E

Marking pins

Stuffing

8 Make the face

First, sew the outline of the nose, then fill it in with straight stitches. To finish, pull the thread out where the ear on the opposite side joins the head, make a French knot, and scoop up one stitch before cutting the thread.

Trim the pile

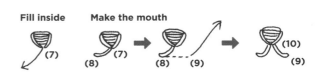

Outline of nose

(2)
(1)
→
(2) (3)
(1) (4)
→
(5)
(4)
→
(5) (6)

Fill inside

(7)

Make the mouth

(8) (7)
→
(8) (9)
→
(10)
(9)

⑨ Attach the eyes

First, attach the whites of the eyes. Since it's difficult to cut out small parts when holding the fabric, cut out the pieces with a little extra allowance, impale it on a needle or a marking pin, then cut off the excess. (Refer to Instruction Pointer 3). Next, the pupils. Place the white part of the eye to where you would like the eye situated, then insert the needle into the fabric where the ear joins the head and pull out of the head through the center of the white of the eye. Thread an onyx bead and sew it on. Thread it through a couple of times and secure it firmly so that the hole doesn't show.

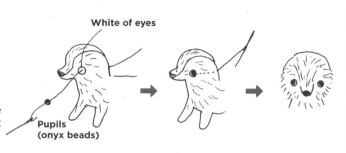

White of eyes

Pupils (onyx beads)

⑩ Attach the ears and the tail

The pattern for the inner ears is slightly smaller. This is so that the ears can curve inwards. With both pieces reverse-side out, stitch edges together except for the base, then turn right-side out. After folding in the edges to curve slightly, use cross-stitches to close. Sew the tail in the similar manner, turn out, and stuff. Don't sew tail closed.

Decide where to put the ears. Sew and secure both edges of the ear then sew from both sides in a curved line, making the ear concave.

Next, attach the tail. Insert the tail into the opening. Add more stuffing to the rear if necessary, then use cross-stitches to secure the tail and sew shut.

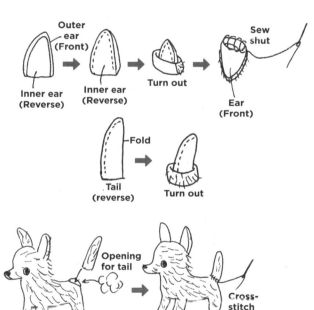

Outer ear (Front)

Inner ear (Reverse)   Inner ear (Reverse)

Turn out

Sew shut

Ear (Front)

Fold

Tail (reverse)   Turn out

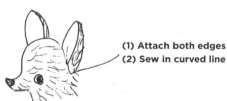

(1) Attach both edges
(2) Sew in curved line

Opening for tail

Cross-stitch

⑪ Finishing

Pull out any pile caught under the seam, brush the coat with a toothbrush, and you're done!

Done!

Hayato & Yamato

Photo
p. 6

Instructions

Shiba Inu:
Hayato & Yamato

These pups are from Japan.
They have short hair and a curled tail.
Don't they look smart?

Yamato

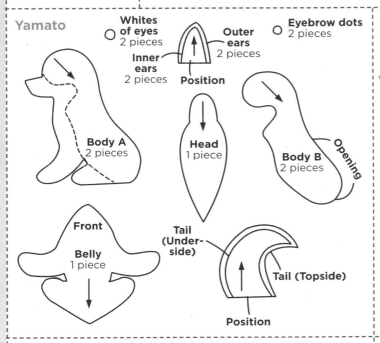

Whites of eyes
2 pieces

Inner ears
2 pieces

Outer ears
2 pieces

Position

Eyebrow dots
2 pieces

Body A
2 pieces

Head
1 piece

Body B
2 pieces

Opening

Front

Belly
1 piece

Tail (Underside)

Tail (Topside)

Position

Hayato

Body A
2 pieces

Body B
2 pieces

Opening

Materials

Yamato
Body B, head, outer ears, tail (topside):
  miniature fur/fleece (shiny black)
Body A, belly, tail (underside): miniature fur/fleece (shiny black)
Inner ears: micro suede (smoky pink)
Eyebrow dots, whites of eyes: micro suede (in white)
Eyes: onyx beads

Hayato
Body B, head, outer ears, tail (topside):
  miniature fur/fleece (shiny light brown)
Body A, belly, tail (underside): miniature fur/fleece (shiny white)
Inner ears: micro suede (smoky pink)
Eyes: onyx beads

Pointers!
Upward curving tail, short ears

Whites of eyes:
  Refer to Instruction Pointer 3
Eyebrow dots:
  Refer to Instruction Pointers 3, 4
Patches:
  Refer to Instruction Pointer 6
Tail: Stuff the tail

Instructions

Siberian Husky:
John

With their blue eyes and gray fur, Siberian Huskies are a popular breed. I hope their owners treat them with lots of love.

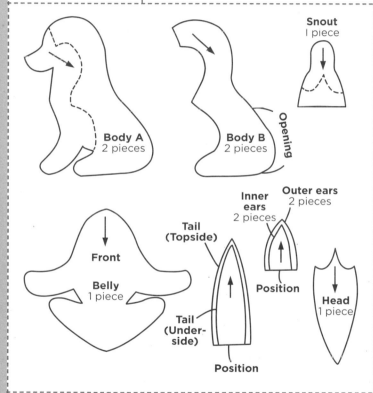

Body A 2 pieces

Body B 2 pieces

Opening

Snout 1 piece

Front

Belly 1 piece

Tail (Topside)

Tail (Underside)

Inner ears 2 pieces

Outer ears 2 pieces

Position

Position

Head 1 piece

How to Attach Glass Eyes

Appx. 2/5" (1 cm)

Cut wires → Make a loop

Put the thread through → Squeeze loop to flatten

Create hole with awl → Insert needle and pull thread tightly

Using a fine-point blue pen, draw lines at corners of eyes

Materials
Body B, head, outer ears, tail (topside):
  miniature fur/fleece (shiny gray)
Snout, body A, belly, tail (underside):
  miniature fur/fleece (shiny white)
Inner ears: ultra suede (pink)
Eyes: glass eyes (in blue) 1/16" (2 mm) in diameter

Pointers!
Blue glass eyes, wide eyes (Draw lines with a blue pen)

Patches:
  Refer to Instruction Pointer 6
Tail: Stuff the tail

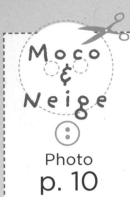

Photo
p. 10

Instructions

Toy Poodles:
Moco & Neige

**These pups are cute as stuffed animals.
Curly hair is the best, don't you think?**

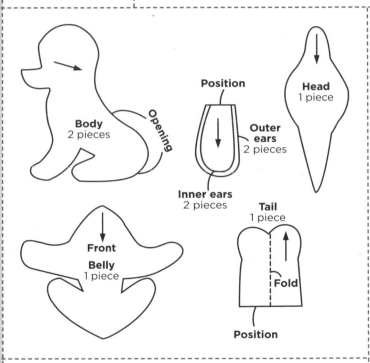

Body
2 pieces

Opening

Position

Outer ears
2 pieces

Inner ears
2 pieces

Head
1 piece

Front
Belly
1 piece

Tail
1 piece

Fold

Position

Finishing

Brush against the pile direction

Materials

Moco
Body, belly, head, outer ears, tail: faux (viscose) fur (brown)
Inner ears: micro suede (dark beige)
Eyes: onyx beads

Neige
Body, belly, head, outer ears, tail: faux (viscose) fur (white)
Inner ears: micro suede (smoky pink)
Eyes: onyx beads

 ## Pointers!
**High forehead, poofy coat
(Brush the coat against the pile direction)**

Treatment of fur:
   Refer to Instruction Pointer 2
Tail: Stuff the tail

Elf

Photo
p. 12

Instructions

Cavalier King Charles Spaniel: Elf

Their faces seem to be always sweetly smiling.
They were the favorite dogs of certain British royals.

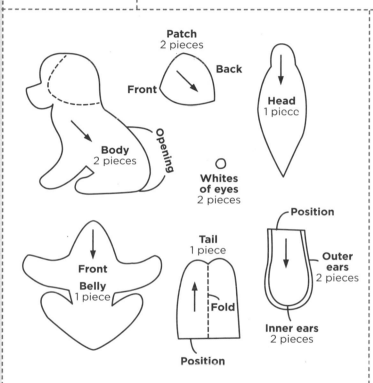

Patch
2 pieces

Front   Back

Head
1 piece

Body
2 pieces

Opening

**Whites
of eyes**
2 pieces

**Front
Belly**
1 piece

Tail
1 piece

Fold

Position

Position

**Outer
ears**
2 pieces

Inner ears
2 pieces

Finishing

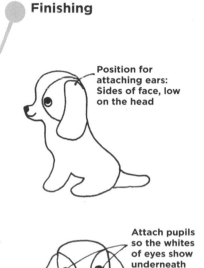

Position for attaching ears:
Sides of face, low on the head

Attach pupils so the whites of eyes show underneath

Materials

Body, belly, head: faux (viscose) fur (white)
Patch, outer ears, tail: faux (viscose) fur (brown)
Inner ears: micro suede (dark beige)
Whites of eyes: micro suede (white)
Eyes: onyx beads

 Pointers!
Upward glance

Treatment of fur:
  Refer to Instruction Pointer 2
Whites of eyes:
  Refer to Instruction Pointer 3
Patches:
  Refer to Instruction Pointer 6
Tail: Stuff the tail

Instructions

Border Collie:
Friday

Collies seem to be good at playing frisbee.
They're excellent athletes. And smart.
But they're mischievous.
Reminds me of a classmate I had one
time... He was popular with the girls.

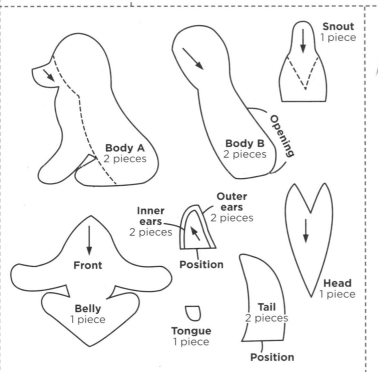

Body A
2 pieces

Body B
2 pieces

Opening

Snout
1 piece

Inner ears
Outer ears
2 pieces

Position

Front

Belly
1 piece

Tongue
1 piece

Tail
2 pieces

Position

Head
1 piece

Finishing

Attach ears at
the corners of the
head and face
them outward.

Materials

Body B, head, outer ears, tail: faux (viscose) fur (black)
Body A, belly, snout: faux (viscose) fur (white)
Inner ears: micro suede (black)
Tongue: micro suede (dark pink)
Eyes: onyx beads

Pointers!
Outward-facing small ears

Treatment of fur:
  Refer to Instruction Pointer 2
Tongue: Refer to Instruction Pointers 3, 4
Patches: Refer to Instruction Pointer 6
Tail: Stuff the tail

Fango

Photo
p. 18

Instructions

Dalmatian:
Fango

**It's not easy to give them spots.
Let's try to make 101 of them!**

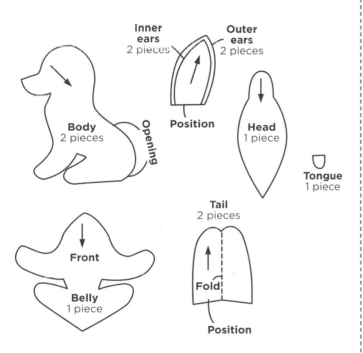

Inner ears
2 pieces

Outer ears
2 pieces

Position

Body
2 pieces

Opening

Head
1 piece

Tongue
1 piece

Front

Belly
1 piece

Tail
2 pieces

Fold

Position

Finishing

Draw dots while paying attention to the overall balance

Pen

Materials

Body, belly, head: miniature fur/fleece (white)
Outer ears: miniature fur/fleece (one each in white and black)
Inner ears: micro suede (smoky pink)
Tail: miniature fur/fleece (black)
Tongue: micro suede (dark pink)
Eyes: onyx beads

Pointers!
**Spots
(Draw randomly with a pen with pigment-based ink)**

Drooping ears:
 Refer to Instruction Pointer 5
Tongue: Refer to Instruction Pointers 3, 4
Tail: Stuff the tail

73

Instructions

Airedale Terrier:
Alex

They have a frank disposition compared to other terriers.
I hear that they are unpredictable—just when you think they're asleep, they suddenly get up and start playing.

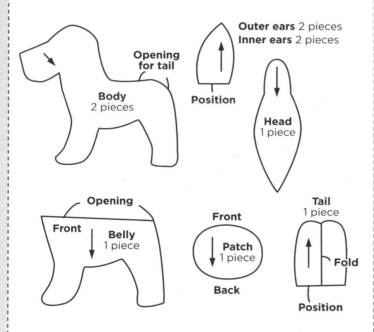

Body 2 pieces

Opening for tail

Position

Outer ears 2 pieces
Inner ears 2 pieces

Head 1 piece

Opening

Front

Belly 1 piece

Front

Patch 1 piece

Back

Tail 1 piece

Fold

Position

How to add ears, patch

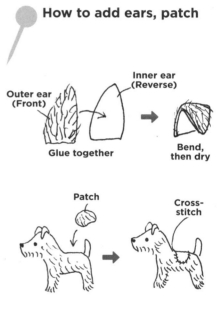

Outer ear (Front)

Inner ear (Reverse)

Glue together

Bend, then dry

Patch

Cross-stitch

Materials
Body, belly, head, outer ears, tail: faux (viscose) fur (brown)
Patch: faux (viscose) fur (black)
Inner ears: micro suede (dark beige)
Eyes: onyx beads

Pointers!
Long snout, patch on back (sew on last using cross-stitches), bent ears (glue together separate pieces, bend in the middle, then dry)

Treatment of fur:
  Refer to Instruction Pointer 2
Tail: Don't stuff the tail

Pocky

Photo
p. 22

Instructions

Yorkshire Terrier:
Pocky

Preppy Yorkies with soft fur in gray and beige.
They're cute, but then again, I hear that they are quite assertive. But I forgive them 'cause they're so cute.

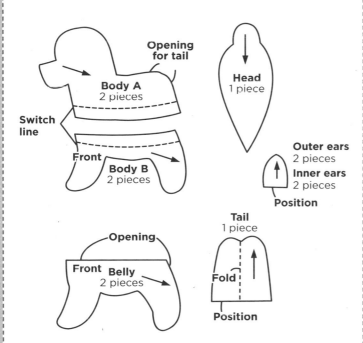

Opening for tail

Body A
2 pieces

Switch line

Front

Body B
2 pieces

Head
1 piece

Outer ears
2 pieces
Inner ears
2 pieces

Position

Opening

Front **Belly**
2 pieces

Tail
1 piece

Fold

Position

Switch Line

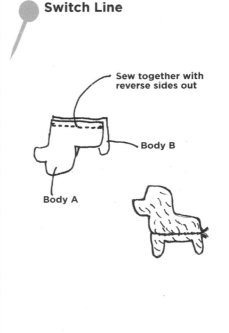

Sew together with reverse sides out

Body B

Body A

Materials

Body A, head, outer ears, tail: faux (viscose) fur (gray)
Body B, Belly: faux (viscose) fur (light beige)
Inner ears: micro suede (dark beige)
Eyes: onyx beads

 ## Pointers!

Body has 2 colors (sew together with reverse sides out), cocked ears (you can get tiny cocked ears by gluing together outer ears and inner ears; let dry, then attach to head.)

Treatment of fur:
   Refer to Instruction Pointer 2
Tail: Stuff the tail

Chappy

Photo
p. 24

Instructions

Maltese:
Chappy

They must know just how cute they are, with the way they look up at you with their softly sparkling eyes.
I think they could write a book titled, "The Reason Why They Spoil Us."

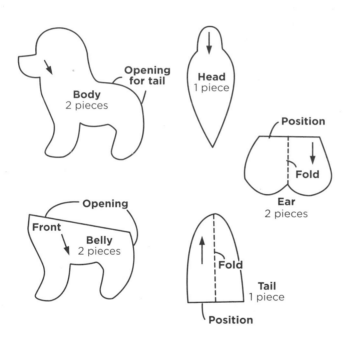

Body
2 pieces

Opening for tail

Head
1 piece

Position

Fold

Ear
2 pieces

Opening

Front

Belly
2 pieces

Fold

Tail
1 piece

Position

Finishing

Part pile on snout at the center, and brush well.

Materials
Body, belly, head, ears, tail: faux (viscose) fur (white)
Eyes: onyx beads

Pointers!
Curled tail

Treatment of fur:
  Refer to Instruction Pointer 2
Tail: Don't stuff the tail.
  Refer to Instruction Pointer 7

Instructions

Bulldog:
Kichijirou

They look ready to pick a fight, but are charmingly disarming. I made the face wrinkles by pulling the fabric back with the thread.

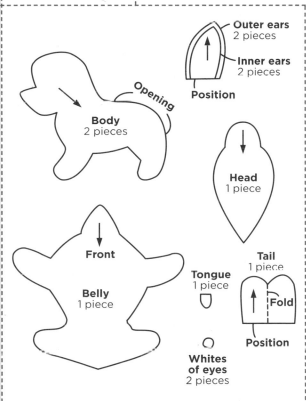

Outer ears
2 pieces

Inner ears
2 pieces

Position

Body
2 pieces

Opening

Head
1 piece

Front

Belly
1 piece

Tongue
1 piece

Tail
1 piece

Fold

Position

Whites of eyes
2 pieces

Instructions

Body: With the reverse sides of the head and body pieces facing out, secure point A (tip of the snout) with a figure-8 knot, and sew together up to point B (back of the head). Sew together the other side up to point C (edge of opening on the back). Next, from point A, sew together the belly (reverse sides out). Turn right-side out, then stuff.

Face: Using a pen with pigment-based ink, draw a patch at the base of one of the eyes. Next, attach the eyes and sew nose. Insert needle from the back of the head, and pull the thread out where you want to place a wrinkle. Push needle back through head starting higher on the forehead, and pull towards the back of the head. Place wrinkles between eyebrows, above the snout. Last, attach the tongue, and draw dots for whiskers.

Finishing: Attach ears and tail, and you're done.

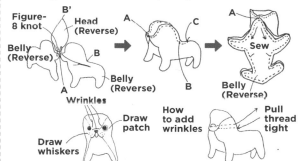

Figure-8 knot

B'

Head (Reverse)

Belly (Reverse)

A

B

A

C

A

Sew

Belly (Reverse)

Belly (Reverse)

B

Wrinkles

Draw patch

How to add wrinkles

Pull thread tight

Draw whiskers

Materials

Body, head, belly: miniature fur/fleece (white)
Tail: miniature fur/fleece (light beige)
Outer ears: miniature fur/fleece
  (1 each in light beige and brown)
Inner ears: micro suede (dark beige)
Tongue: micro suede (dark pink)
Whites of eyes: micro suede (white)
Pupils: onyx beads

Pointers!

Squished-in face (create wrinkles by pulling thread), whiskers and patch around eye (draw with a pen)

Droopy ears: Refer to Instruction Pointer 5
Whites of eyes: Refer to Instruction Pointer 3
Tongue: Refer to Instruction Pointers 3, 4
Tail: Stuff the tail

Noel

Photo
p. 28

Instructions

Japanese Spitz:
Noel

**They're No. 1 on my list of dogs that I want to own.
I always assumed that they were a type of Pomeranian.**

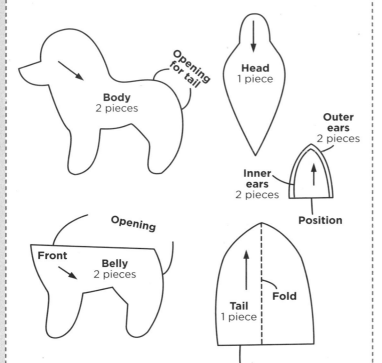

Body
2 pieces

Opening for tail

Head
1 piece

Outer ears
2 pieces

Inner ears
2 pieces

Position

Opening

Front

Belly
2 pieces

Tail
1 piece

Fold

Position

Treatment of fabric at the tips of snout and legs

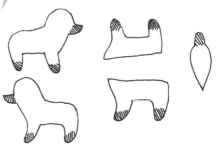

▨ **Trim fur in the shaded areas**

Sew together after trimming the pile at the tip of the snout and the feet.

Materials
Body, belly, head, outer ears, tail: straight mohair fabric (white)
Inner ears: ultra suede (pink)
Eyes: onyx beads

Pointers!
Curled tail

Treatment of fur:
    Refer to Instruction Pointer 2
Tail: Don't stuff the tail.
    Refer to Instruction Pointer 7

Cute Pups
Canine Friends and Accessories

Translation: Molly Kiser

Published by Vertical, Inc., New York.

Originally published in Japanese as
Mamemame Gekijyo, Mamewanko
by Bunka Shuppankyoku, Tokyo, 2002.

ISBN 978-1-934287-68-2

Manufactured in The United States of America

First American Edition

Vertical, Inc.
www.vertical-inc.com

Afterword

Time flew after my first book, *Cute Dogs*, was published.
A whole year passed very quickly.
Although I'm basically lazy and careless,
I was able to produce a really fun book thanks to the
encouraging support that I received from my friends and
associates.
For the photo shoots, other than the things that I made
myself, Ms. Kiyomi Ito from the Mizuiro Studio contributed
yummy-looking cookies, hamburgers, a star-patterned
sofa, glasses, wooden toys, etc., which added a great
atmosphere to the pups' photos.
I hope that you enjoy the "tiny, tiny world" enhanced by
these little accessories.

Chie Hayano

Born in 1971. She loves handcrafting, drawing pictures, and small things.
She started making miniature stuffed animals in
1998. Participated in miniature craft competitions
under the name "Soramame Studio." She has also
presented her work on her website. Her aim is to
create works with presense which, even if they're
small, expand people's imaginations.

Soramame Studio
http://www01.u-page.so-net.ne.jp/zd5/soramame/